Summer of 1969

The Story of Cozett Juanita Gambrel

Written by

JUANITA G. FLOYD and SARA W. BERRY

Illustrated by Tracy Applewhite

Copyright © 2017 by Sara W. Berry

All rights reserved. This book is protected under the copyright laws of the United States of America, and may not be reproduced in any format without written permission from the author.

ISBN: 978-0-9841261-2-5
Printed in the United States of America

Illustrator:
Tracy Applewhite
www.tracyapplewhite.com

Sara W. Berry's Author Photograph:
Stephanie Rhea
www.stephanierhea.com

Juanita G. Floyd's Author Photograph:
Lisa Browning
www.LisaBrowningPhotography.com

Published by
Integrity Time, LLC
P.O. Box 7286
Tupelo, MS 38802
www.integritytime.com

Dedicated to the memory of

**Mrs. Bernice Wade Gambrel,
an unsung hero**

In 1969,

the United States began the historical process of desegregation.

Black children and white children, who were once educated in

separate settings, began attending schools together. This is one

young girl's true story about her experiences during that transition.

Today, we celebrate the changes which have occurred, and we look

longingly for continued integration of our lives together.

It was summer of '69, and school had just let out.
I was playing outside when I heard Mama shout.

"Juanita, come here!" I heard loud and clear.
I turned toward the house and saw her walk near.

I saw an envelope in her right hand.
"Tell me your name," she said in command.

"My name is Juanita, you know that full well.
So why is it now you want me to tell?"

Well, sassy behavior she never did like,
And the look that she gave me did cause quite a fright.

"Juanita," I said with a bit more respect.
"Tell me your full name," she then did direct.

"Cozett Juanita Gambrel," I calmly did say.
Then she gave me a hug and sent me back out to play.

"What is your name?" she asked the next day.
"Why, you know my name," with a smile I did say.

"Tell me your full name, say it loud and clear."
"Cozett Juanita Gambrel!" I said so the neighbors could hear.

She gave me a hug and then she did turn,
but not before I saw her look of concern.

Each day the questions, they all were the same.
And I began to tire of my mother's new game.

"What is your name?" she asked once again.
"Juanita," I said, with a wide, loose-tooth grin.

"Tell me your full name, tell me right now."
"Cozett Juanita Gambrel," I said with a scowl.

"There may come a time when new places you'll go.
There may come a time you are glad that you know."

That's all my mom said as she turned to the house.
I stood there, just thinking, as still as a mouse.

Of course I know my name, what is she saying?
Then I shrugged off those thoughts and continued my playing.

Throughout that hot summer, my mom acted strange.
I hoped this behavior wasn't permanent change.

She worked in our garden each day after work,
And I'd always convinced her her duties to shirk.

She'd put down the rake, the seeds, and the spade.
And we'd laugh and have fun, and till dark we played.

But that, too, had changed and I didn't know why.
I asked her to play, but "No" was the reply.

"Why don't you sit there under the tree,
And read your books, and let me be."

My mother kept quiet, simply dug in the dirt.
She never did notice my eyes full of hurt.

That whole summer, it all was the same.
I read all my books and said my full name.

The night before school began once again,
My mother came close and took my small hand.

"Juanita, my love, your school will be new.
The children there are not like you.

Their skin is white and yours is quite brown,
But all children are special deep down.

But trust me, my love, the differences are few,
And soon your new friends will love you for you.

But don't be discouraged, it may take a while
For them to see past your skin to your great big smile."

She knew I might hear words that would sting
Words that were untrue, just downright mean.

But she prayed each day that I would not do the same,
But turn my brown cheek and remember my name.

The first day of school came way too soon,
And my mother walked with me to my new room.

She greeted the teacher and then cleared her throat
"Teacher, I trust you," were the words that she spoke.

"I believe you'll protect her, this daughter of mine.
I believe you will love her and teach her just fine."

She let go of my hand and walked out the door.
She turned back just once to say a bit more.

"Just one request, Teacher, if you don't mind.
My child likes her books; she reads all the time.

Here is her satchel of books brought from home.
Could she take them to recess, in case she's alone?"

In all of the class I was the only black one.
Still, I thought, we could all have fun.

But the things my mother had feared soon came true
And the children wouldn't play with the brown girl who was new.

Some called me names, which were vicious and mean,
But I remembered my mom's teaching and on truth I would lean.

"That's not my name, it's simply untrue.
Don't call me mean names because I am new."

"Cozett Juanita Gambrel, that is my name.
And if you ask me again, I'll tell you the same."

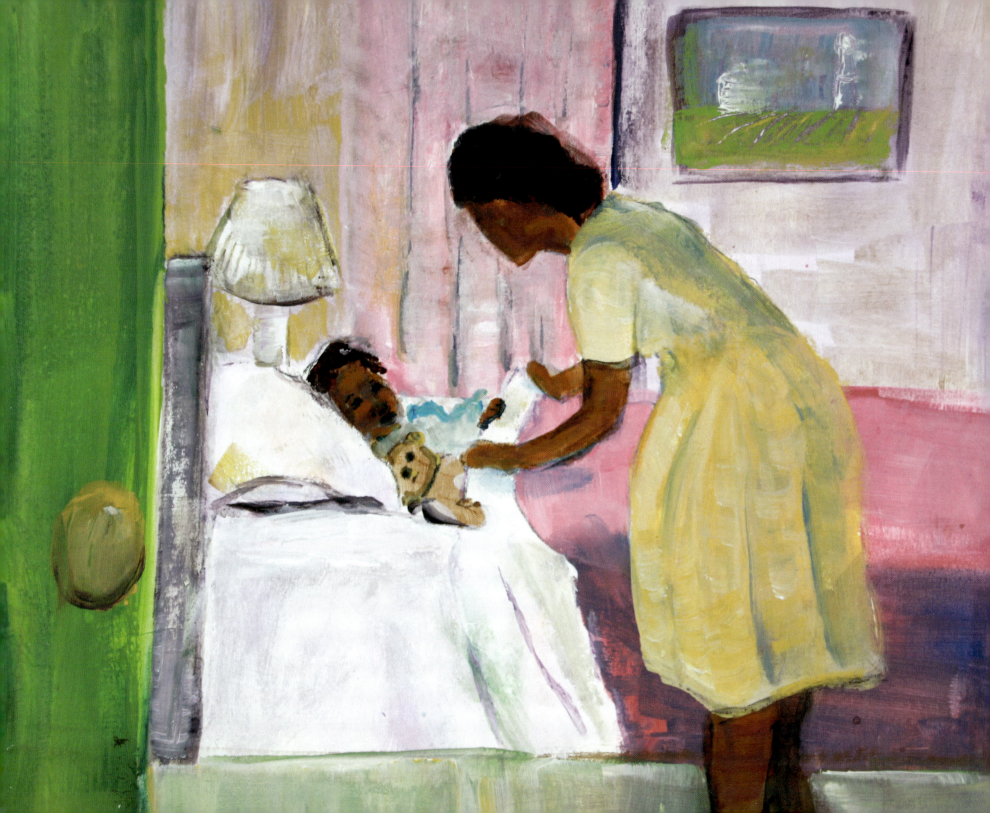

When I'd tell Mama what happened during recess at school,
She'd always remind me of the Golden Rule.

"You just treat others like you wish they would do.
Be sure to treat them as you wish they'd treat you."

"Give it some time," my mother would say.
"These are children, like you. They will want to play."

As time went on, I put down my books.
I no longer endured the terrible looks.

They saw me for me, saw past my skin.
They saw me for me, to what was within.

And I saw past theirs, I'm happy to say,
and soon at recess we began to play.

Those little white children became my dear friends.
We saw past the difference; we saw past the skin.

For ten years we grew together at school,
And each to the other extended the Golden Rule.

"Juanita for office!" And they held up a sign.
Their white hands raised high, these dear friends of mine.

My mother was right, as was always the case.
All children are special, no matter the race.

We are all challenged...

to reflect on who has inspired and influenced us; and we are wise to ask ourselves how are we influencing others. Many times, role models, mentors, friends, and heroes are not always the most well-known or well educated, yet their encouragement becomes the inspiration for us to succeed. I acknowledge that there have been many influences in my life, but the one who inspired me the most was my mother, Mrs. Bernice Gambrel, an unsung hero.

She was my motivator, my teacher, a strong proponent of family and family values, and sole provider for the family of seven children after the untimely death of my father when I was young. My mother always worked hard at her jobs and worked overtime to support her children and grandchildren. Her wisdom far exceeded her eighth-grade education.

Wilma Rudolf, the Olympic track star said, "The doctor told me I would never walk, but my mother told me I could—so I believed my mother."

My mother instilled in me great confidence and values. My mother's wisdom extended into many areas, and I know it's because of my mother's influence that I have a college degree and a wonderful career. My mother constantly said to me, "You can do it. You can achieve it. You can be successful. You can be anything you want to be in life!"

Many times, role models, mentors, friends, and heroes are not always the most well-known or well educated, yet their encouragement becomes the inspiration for us to succeed

How does a mother prepare a child for difficult circumstances? How does a mother create an unshakeable confidence in her children? My mother knew how. In the summer of 1969, the pivotal year of school integration, I had just finished 1st grade at B.F. Ford Elementary in New Albany, Mississippi. That summer, my mother told me I was going to a new school for 2nd grade.

"Will my friends be there?" I asked.

"Probably not, but you will make new friends," she answered.

With great wisdom, my mother constantly told me, "You will be a light. You will love. You will not hate."

My mother's teachings of love remind me of the words of Howard Thurman many years ago:

"If we love a child, and the child senses that we love him, he will get a concept of love that all the subsequent hatred in the world will never be able to destroy."

That is the kind of love my mother showed me and taught me to show others.

That is the kind of love I challenge you to show to others in your sphere of influence.

If we all show that kind of love, we just might change the world—together.

- Cozett Juanita Gambrel Floyd

*Juanita and her mother,
Mrs. Bernice Wade Gambrel*

JUANITA G. FLOYD is Vice-President of Finance and Administration for CREATE Foundation and is a popular inspirational speaker and columnist. Juanita is a graduate of Northeast Mississippi Community College and The University of Mississippi with a Bachelor's Degree in Accounting. Her siblings are Ray, Barbara, Wade, Valerie and Frank. She is the proud parent of three wonderful children, Tyler, Taylor and Tyra and one grandson, Andrew.

SARA W. BERRY is a wife, a mother, an author, a speaker, and a teacher. She is a graduate of Millsaps College in Jackson, Mississippi, where she received a Bachelor of Science Degree in Education. She is married to Dr. Mont Berry and is mother to seven incredible children and two wonderful sons-in-law, Katie and Owen, Ellie and Drew, Joseph, Troy, Joshua, Sally, and Charlie.

TRACY APPLEWHITE BROOME is a fine artist and illustrator. She enjoys working with inspirational authors such as the authors of this book. She resides on the lovely Mississippi Gulf Coast with her family. Tracy is passionate about painting images that communicate faith and hope.

Wise Words from Martin Luther King, Jr.

Darkness cannot drive out darkness; only light can do that. Hate cannot drive out hate; only love can do that.

The ultimate measure of a man is not where he stands in moments of comfort and convenience, but where he stands at times of challenge and controversy.

I look to a day when people will not be judged by the color of their skin, but by the content of their character.

I have decided to stick with love. Hate is too great a burden to bear.

We must learn to live together as brothers or perish together as fools.